Mark Fiore's

Heroes of Greek Mythology

Mark Fiore's

Heroes of Greek Mythology

Illustrated by

Mark Fiore

Written by

Joel Skidmore

Based on Homer's *Odyssey*, the *Library* of Apollodorus, and secondary sources, especially Edward Tripp's *Meridian Handbook of Classical Mythology*. Pronunciation of Greek names follows the conventions of the great English poets.

ISBN 978-1-7350606-4-4

© 2024 Mythweb

Contents

If a hero is properly defined as someone who does something dangerous to help somebody else, then the heroes of Greek mythology do not qualify. They were a pretty selfish bunch, often with additional antisocial tendencies thrown into the bargain — in other words, not exactly role models for the younger generation of today. But knowing their names and exploits is essential for understanding references in literature and even popular culture today. So let's recognize and celebrate Hercules and Perseus and the others by their proper dictionary definition: "In mythology and legend, a man or woman, often of divine ancestry, who is endowed with great courage and strength, celebrated for his or her bold exploits, and favored by the gods."

Heracles

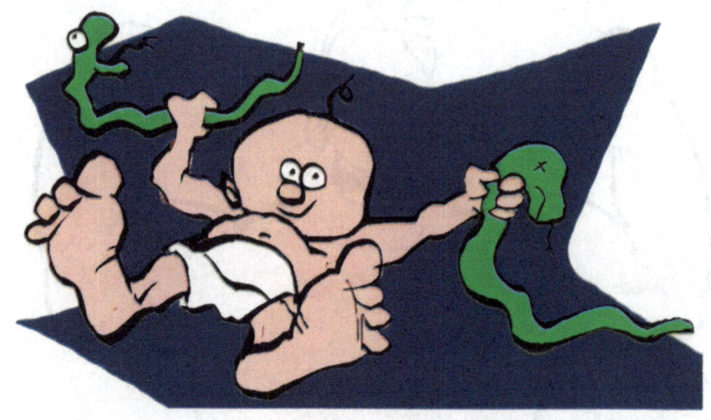

Birth

Hercules was the Roman name for Heracles, the greatest hero of Greek mythology. Like most authentic heroes, Heracles had a god as one of his parents, being the son of the supreme deity Zeus and a mortal woman. Zeus's queen Hera was jealous of Heracles, and when he was still an infant she sent two snakes to kill him in his crib. Heracles was found prattling delighted baby talk, a strangled serpent in each hand.

Pronunciation:
Heracles (HER-a-kleez), Zeus (zyoos or zoos), Hera (HEE-ruh)

The Labors

When he had come of age and already proved himself an unerring marksman with a bow and arrow, a champion wrestler and the possessor of superhuman strength, Heracles was driven mad by Hera. In a frenzy, he killed his own children. To atone for this crime, he was sentenced to perform a series of tasks, or "Labors", for his cousin Eurystheus, the king of Tiryns and Mycenae. By rights, Hercules should have been king himself, but Hera had tricked her husband Zeus into crowning Eurystheus instead.

Eurystheus (yoo-RIS-thyoos), Tiryns (TIR-inz),
Mycenae (mye-SEE-nee)

Labor One The Nemean Lion

As his first Labor, Heracles was challenged to kill the Nemean lion. This was no easy feat, for the beast's parentage was supernatural and it was more of a monster than an ordinary lion. Its skin could not be penetrated by spears or arrows. Heracles blocked off the entrances to the lion's cave, crawled into the close confines where it would have to fight face to face, and throttled it to death with his bare hands. Ever afterwards he wore the lion's skin as a cloak and its gaping jaws as a helmet.

Nemean (nee-MEE-un)

Labor Two **The Hydra**

King Eurystheus was so afraid of his heroic cousin that when he saw him coming with the Nemean lion on his shoulder, he hid in a storage jar. From this shelter he issued the order for the next Labor. Heracles was to seek out and destroy the monstrous and many-headed Hydra. The mythmakers agree that the Hydra lived in the swamps of Lerna, but they seem to have had trouble counting its heads. Some said that the Hydra had eight or nine, while others claimed as many as ten thousand. All agreed, however, that as soon as one head was beaten down or chopped off, two more grew in its place.

Hydra (HYE-druh), Lerna (LUR-nuh)

Labor Two The Hydra (continued)

To make matters worse, the Hydra's very breath was lethal. Even smelling its footprints was enough to kill an ordinary mortal. Fortunately, Heracles was no ordinary mortal. He sought out the monster in its lair and brought it out into the open with flaming arrows. But now the fight went in the Hydra's favor. It twined its many heads around the hero and tried to trip him up. It called on an ally, a huge crab that also lived in the swamp. The crab bit Heracles in the heel and further impeded his attack. Heracles was on the verge of failure when he remembered his nephew, Iolaus, the son of his twin brother Iphicles.

Iolaus (eye-oh-LAY-us), Iphicles (IF-i-kleez)

Labor Two **The Hydra (concluded)**

Iolaus, who had driven Heracles to Lerna in a chariot, looked on in anxiety as his uncle became entangled in the Hydra's snaky heads. Finally he could bear it no longer. In response to his uncle's shouts, he grabbed a burning torch and dashed into the fray. Now, as soon as Heracles cut off one of the Hydra's heads, Iolaus was there to sear the wounded neck with flame. This kept further heads from sprouting. Heracles cut off the heads one by one, with Iolaus cauterizing the wounds. Finally Heracles lopped off the one head that was supposedly immortal and buried it deep beneath a rock.

Iolaus (eye-oh-LAY-us)

Labor Three The Cerynitian Hind

The third Labor was the capture of the Cerynitian hind. Though a female deer, this fleet-footed beast had golden horns. It was sacred to Artemis, goddess of the hunt, so Heracles dared not wound it. He hunted it for an entire year before running it down on the banks of the River Ladon in Arcadia. Taking careful aim with his bow, he fired an arrow between the tendons and bones of the two forelegs, pinning it down without drawing blood. All the same, Artemis was displeased, but Heracles dodged her wrath by blaming his taskmaster Eurystheus.

Cerynitian (sur-ih-NISH-iun), Artemis (AR-ti-mis), Ladon (LAY-don), Arcadia (ar-KAY-dee-uh)

Labor Four **The Erymanthian Boar**

The fourth Labor took Heracles back to Arcadia in quest of an enormous boar, which he was challenged to bring back alive. While tracking it down he stopped to visit the centaur Pholus. This creature — half-horse, half-man — was examining one of the hero's arrows when he accidentally dropped it on his foot. Because it had been soaked in poisonous Hydra venom, Pholus succumbed immediately. Heracles finally located the boar on Mount Erymanthus and managed to drive it into a snowbank, immobilizing it. Flinging it up onto his shoulder, he carried it back to Eurystheus, who cowered as usual in his storage jar.

Pholus (FOH-lus), Erymanthus (er-ih-MAN-thus)

Labor Five The Augean Stables

Eurystheus was very pleased with himself for dreaming up the next Labor, which he was sure would humiliate his heroic cousin. Heracles was to clean out the stables of King Augeas in a single day. Augeas possessed vast herds of cattle which had deposited their manure in such quantity over the years that a thick aroma hung over the entire Peloponnesus. Instead of employing a shovel and a basket as Eurystheus imagined, Heracles diverted two rivers through the stableyard and got the job done without getting dirty. But because he had demanded payment of Augeas, Eurystheus refused to count this as a Labor.

Augeas (aw-JEE-us), Peloponnesus (pel-i-po-NEE-sus)

Labor Six **The Stymphalian Birds**

The sixth Labor pitted Heracles against the Stymphalian birds, who inhabited a marsh near Lake Stymphalus in Arcadia. The sources differ as to whether these birds feasted on human flesh, killed men by shooting them with feathers of brass, or merely constituted a nuisance because of their number. Heracles could not approach the birds to fight them — the ground was too swampy to bear his weight and too mucky to wade through. Finally he resorted to some castanets given to him by the goddess Athena. By making a racket with these, he caused the birds to take wing. And once they were in the air, he brought them down by the dozens with his arrows.

Stymphalian (stim-FAY-lee-un), Stymphalus (stim-FAY-lus), Athena (a-THEE-nuh)

Labor Seven The Cretan Bull

Queen Pasiphae of Crete had been inspired by a vengeful god to fall in love with a bull, with the result that the Minotaur was born — a monster half-man and half-bull that haunted the Labyrinth of King Minos. Pasiphae's husband was understandably eager to be rid of the bull, which was also ravaging the Cretan countryside, so Hercules was assigned the task as his seventh Labor. Although the beast belched flames, the hero overpowered it and shipped it back to the mainland. It ended up near Athens, where it became the duty of another hero, Theseus, to deal with it once more.

Pasiphae (pa-SIF-ay-ee), Crete (kreet), Minotaur (MIN-uh-tawr), Labyrinth (LAB-i-rinth), Minos (MYE-nos)

Labor Eight The Mares of Diomedes

Next Heracles was instructed to bring Eurystheus the mares of Diomedes. These horses dined on the flesh of travelers who made the mistake of accepting Diomedes' hospitality. In one version of the myth, Heracles pacified the beasts by feeding them their own master. In another, they satisfied their appetites on the hero's squire, a young man named Abderus. In any case, Heracles soon rounded them up and herded them down to sea, where he embarked them for Tiryns. Once he had shown them to Eurystheus, he released them. They were eventually eaten by wild animals on Mount Olympus.

Diomedes (dye-uh-MEE-deez), Abderus (AB-de-rus)

Labor Nine **Hippolyte's Belt**

The ninth Labor took Heracles to the land of the Amazons, to retrieve the belt of their queen for Eurystheus' daughter. The Amazons were a race of warrior women, great archers who had invented the art of fighting from horseback. Heracles recruited a number of heroes to accompany him on this expedition, among them Theseus. As it turned out, the Amazon queen, Hippolyte, willingly gave Hercules her belt, but Hera was not about to let the hero get off so easily. The goddess stirred up the Amazons with a rumor that the Greeks had captured their queen, and a great battle ensued. Heracles made off with the belt, and Theseus kidnapped an Amazon princess.

Theseus (THEES-yoos or THEE-see-us), Hippolyte (hi-POL-i-tee)

Labor Ten The Cattle of Geryon

In creating monsters and formidable foes, the Greek mythmakers used a simple technique of multiplication. Thus Geryon, the owner of some famous cattle that Heracles was now instructed to steal, had three heads and/or three separate bodies from the waist down. His watchdog, Orthrus, had only two heads. This Labor took place somewhere in the country we know as Spain. The hound Orthrus rushed at Heracles as he was making off with the cattle, and the hero killed him with a single blow from the wooden club which he customarily carried. Geryon was dispatched as well, and Heracles drove the herd back to Greece, taking a wrong turn along the way and passing through Italy.

Geryon (GAIR-ee-un), Orthrus (OR-thrus)

Labor Eleven **The Apples of the Hesperides**

The Hesperides were nymphs entrusted by the goddess Hera with certain apples which she had received as a wedding present. These were kept in a grove surrounded by a high wall and guarded by Ladon, a many-headed dragon. The grove was located in the far-western mountains named for Atlas, one of the Titans or first generation of gods. Atlas had sided with one of his brothers in a war against Zeus. In punishment, he was compelled to support the weight of the heavens by means of a pillar on his shoulders. Heracles, in quest of the apples, had been told that he would never get the them without the aid of Atlas.

Hesperides (hes-PER-i-deez), Ladon (LAY-don)

Labor Eleven

The Apples of the Hesperides (continued)

The The Titan was only too happy to oblige. He told the hero to hold the pillar while he went to retrieve the fruit. But first Heracles had to kill the dragon by means of an arrow over the garden wall. Atlas soon returned with the apples but now realized how nice it was not to have to strain for eternity keeping heaven and earth apart. Heracles wondered if Atlas would mind taking back the pillar just long enough for him to fetch a cushion for his shoulder. The Titan obliged and Heracles strolled off, neglecting to return.

Labor Twelve **The Capture of Cerberus**

As his final Labor, Heracles was instructed to bring the hellhound Cerberus up from Hades, the kingdom of the dead. The first barrier to the soul's journey beyond the grave was the most famous river of the Underworld, the Styx. Here the newly dead congregated as insubstantial shades, mere wraiths of their former selves, awaiting passage in the ferryboat of Charon the Boatman. Charon wouldn't take anyone across unless they met two conditions. Firstly, they had to pay a bribe in the form of a coin under the corpse's tongue. And secondly, they had to be dead. Heracles met neither condition, a circumstance which aggravated Charon's natural grouchiness.

Cerberus (SUR-buh-rus), Hades (HAY-deez), Styx (stiks), Charon (CARE-on)

Labor Twelve The Capture of Cerberus (continued)

But Heracles simply glowered so fiercely that Charon meekly conveyed him across the Styx. The greater challenge was Cerberus, who had razor teeth, three (or maybe fifty) heads, a venomous snake for a tail, and another swarm of snakes growing out of his back. These lashed at Heracles while Cerberus lunged for a purchase on his throat. Fortunately, the hero was wearing his trusty lion's skin, which was impenetrable by anything short of a thunderbolt from Zeus. Heracles eventually choked Cerberus into submission and dragged him to Tiryns, where he received due credit for this final Labor.

Death

Heracles had a great many other adventures, in after years as well as in between his Labors. It was poisonous Hydra venom that eventually brought about his demise. He had allowed a centaur to ferry his wife Deianeira across a river, and the centaur had attacked her on the other side. Heracles killed him with an arrow, but before he died he told Deianeira to keep some of his blood for a love potion. Deianeira used some on Heracles' tunic to keep him faithful, little realizing that it had been poisoned with Hydra venom from the arrow. Heracles donned the tunic and died in agony.

Deianeira (dee-i-NYE-ruh)

Afterlife

Heracles was the only hero to become a full-fledged god upon his demise, but even in his case there was his mortal aspect to be dealt with. By virtue of his spectacular achievements, even by heroic standards, he was given a home on Mount Olympus and a goddess for a wife. But part of him had come not from his father Zeus but from his mortal mother Alcmene, and that part was sent to the Underworld. As a phantasm it eternally roams the Elysian Fields in the company of other heroes.

Alcmene (alk-MEE-nee), Elysian (ee-LEE-zhun)

Jason

Jason was the son of a king whose brother had usurped the throne. Jason's uncle, whose name was Pelias, lived in constant fear of losing what he had taken so unjustly. He kept Jason's father a prisoner and would certainly have murdered Jason at birth. But Jason's mother deceived Pelias by mourning as if Jason had died. Meanwhile the infant was bundled off to the wilderness cave of Chiron the Centaur. This combination horse-and-man tutored Jason in the lore of plants, the hunt, and the civilized arts. When he had come of age, Jason set out like a proper hero to claim his rightful throne.

Pronunciation: Pelias (PEL-ee-us), Chiron (KYE-ron)

Unknowingly, Jason was to play his part in a plan hatched on lofty Mount Olympus, home of the twelve supreme gods. Hera, queen of the Olympian deities, nursed a rage against King Pelias. For Jason's uncle, the usurper king, had honored all the gods but Hera. Rashly had he begrudged the queen of heaven her due. Hera's plan was fraught with danger; it would require a true hero. To test Jason's mettle, she contrived it that he came to a raging torrent on his way to reclaim his kingdom. And on the bank was a withered old woman. Would Jason go about his business impatiently, or would he give way to her request to be ferried across the stream?

Hera (HEE-ruh)

Jason did not think twice. Taking the crone on his back, he set off into the current. And halfway across he began to stagger under her unexpected weight. For the old woman was none other than Hera in disguise. Some say that she revealed herself to Jason on the far shore; others claim that he never learned of the divine service he had performed. Jason had lost a sandal in the swift-moving stream, and this would prove significant. For an oracle had warned King Pelias, "Beware a stranger who wears but a single sandal." When Jason arrived in his home kingdom, he asserted his claim to the throne. But his uncle Pelias had no intention of giving it up, particularly to a one-shoed stranger.

Under the guise of hospitality, he invited Jason to a banquet. And during the course of the meal, he engaged him in conversation. "You say you've got what it takes to rule a kingdom," said Pelias. "May I take it that you're fit to deal with any thorny problems that arise? For example, how would you go about getting rid of someone who was giving you a pain in the neck?" Jason considered for a moment, eager to show a kingly knack for problem solving. "Send him to barbarian Colchis in quest of the Golden Fleece?" he suggested. "Not a bad idea," responded Pelias. "It's just the sort of quest that any hero worth his salt would leap at. Why, if he succeeded he'd be remembered down through the ages. Tell you what, why don't you go?"

Colchis (KOL-kis)

And so it came to pass that word went out the length and breadth of Greece that Jason was looking for shipmates to embark upon a perilous but glamorous adventure. And in spite of the miniscule chances of anyone surviving to lay eyes upon the Fleece let alone get past the guarding dragon and return with the prize, large numbers of heroes were ready to run the risk. These were known as the Argonauts, after their ship, the Argo. Among them were Hercules — or Heracles, to give him his proper Greek name — and the heroine Atalanta. Jason had the vessel constructed by the worthy shipwright Argus, who in a fit of vanity named her more or less after himself.

Heracles (HER-a-kleez)

Argus had divine sponsorship in his task, Hera having enlisted the aid of her fellow goddess Athena. This patroness of crafts secured a prow for the vessel from timber hewn at the sacred grove of Zeus, king of the Olympian gods. This prow had the magical property of speaking — and prophesying — in a human voice. And so one bright autumn morning the Argo set out to sea, her benches crewed by lusty ranks of heroic rowers. And true to Pelias's fondest aspirations, it wasn't long before big troubles assailed the company. After stopping for better than a fortnight on an island populated exclusively by women, they put in at the kingdom of Salmydessus.

Salmydessus (sal-mih-DES-us)

The king welcomed them but was in no mood for festive entertainment. Because he'd offended the gods, he'd been set upon by woman-headed, bird-bodied, razor-clawed scourges known as Harpies. These Harpies were possessed of reprehensible table manners. Every evening at dinnertime, they dropped by to defecate upon the king's repast and hung around making such a racket that he would not have been able to eat had he the stomach for it. As a result, the king grew thinner by the hour. Fortunately two of Jason's crew were direct descendants of the North Wind, which gave them the power to fly. And they kindly chased the Harpies so far away that the king was never bothered again.

In thanks, the king informed the Argonauts of a danger just ahead on the route to the Golden Fleece — two rocks called the Symplegades, which crashed together upon any ship passing between them. The king even suggested a mechanism by which one might avoid the effects of these Clashing Rocks. If a bird could be induced to pass between the crags first, causing them to clash together, the Argo could follow quickly behind, passing through safely before they were ready to snap shut again. By means of this device, Jason caused the rocks to spring together prematurely, nipping only the tail feathers of the bird. The Argo was able to pass between them relatively unscathed. Only her very stern was splintered.

Symplegades (sim-PLEG-uh-deez)

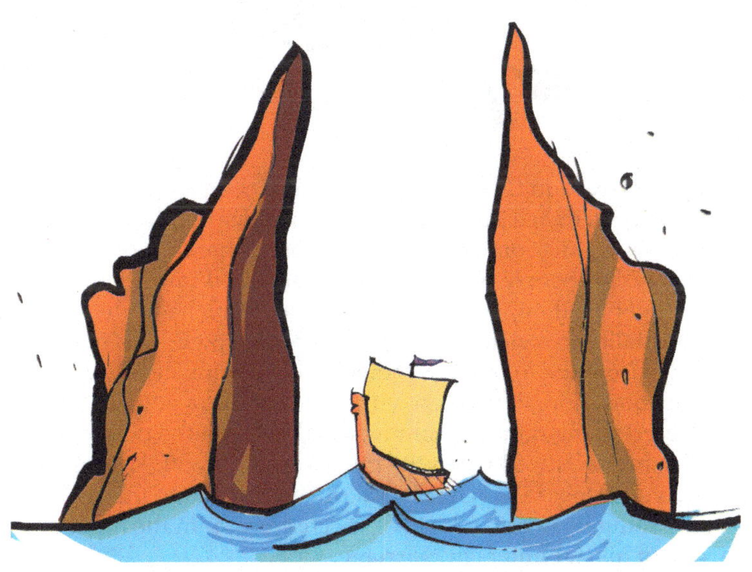

Once arrived in Colchis, Jason had to face a series of challenges meted out by King Aeetes, ruler of this barbarian kingdom on the far edge of the heroic world. He and his people were not kindly disposed toward strangers, although on an earlier occasion he had extended hospitality to a visitor from Jason's home town. This may have been due to the newcomer's unorthodox mode of transportation. For he arrived on the back of a golden-fleeced flying ram. The stranger had been on the point of being sacrificed when the ram carried him off. Having arrived safely in Colchis, he sacrificed the ram to the gods and hung its fleece in a grove. Aeetes gave him the hand of one of his daughters in marriage.

Aeetes (ee-EE-teez)

King Aeetes had taken a disliking to Jason on sight. He had no particular fondness for handsome young strangers who came traipsing into his kingdom on glorious quests featuring the trampling of his sacred grove and the carrying off of his personal property. For King Aeetes considered the Golden Fleece to be his own, and he was in the midst of telling Jason just what he could do with his precious quest when he was reminded of the obligations of hospitality by another of his daughters named Medea. Medea was motivated by more than good manners. For Hera had been looking out for Jason's interests, and she had succeeded in persuading Aphrodite, the goddess of love, to intervene on Jason's behalf.

Aphrodite (a-fro-DYE-tee)

It was no problem at all for Aphrodite to arrange that Medea be stricken with passion for Jason the moment she first saw him. And it was a good thing for Jason that this was so. For not only was he spared a kingly tongue-lashing and a quick trip to the frontier, but Medea quietly offered to help him in his latest predicament. For once her father had calmed down, he had waxed suspiciously reasonable. Of course Jason could have the Fleece and anything else he required in furtherance of his quest — Aeetes couldn't imagine what had possessed him to be so uncooperative. All he required of Jason as a simple token of good faith was the merest of farmyard chores.

There were two bulls standing in the adjacent pasture. If Jason would be so kind as to harness them, plow the field, sow it and reap the harvest in a single day, King Aeetes would be much obliged — and only too happy to turn over the Golden Fleece. Oh, and there was one trifling detail of which Jason should be aware. These bulls were a bit unusual in that their feet were made of brass sharp enough to rip open a man from gullet to gizzard. And then of course there was the matter of their bad breath. In point of fact, they breathed flames. Along about this juncture Jason thought he heard his mommy, Queen Polymede, calling. But then, as noted, Medea took him gently aside and suggested that she might be of aid.

Quite conveniently for Jason, Medea was a famous sorceress, magic potions being her stock in trade. She slipped Jason a salve which, when smeared on his body, made him proof against fire and brazen hooves. And so it was that Jason boldly approached the bulls and brooked no bullish insolence. Disregarding the flames that played merrily about his shoulders and steering clear of the hooves, he forced the creatures into harness and set about plowing the field. Nor was the subsequent sowing any great chore for the now-heartened hero. Gaily strewing seed about like a nymph flinging flowers in springtime, he did not stop to note the unusual nature of the seed.

Aeetes, it turns out, had got his hands on some dragon's teeth with unique agricultural properties. As soon as these hit the soil they began to sprout, which was good from the point of view of Jason accomplishing his task by nightfall, but bad in terms of the harvest. For each seed germinated into a fully-armed warrior, who popped up from the ground and joined the throng now menacing poor Jason. Aeetes, meanwhile, was standing off to the side of the field chuckling quietly to himself. It irked the king somewhat to see his daughter slink across the furrows to Jason's side, but he didn't think too much of it at the time. Having proven herself polite to a fault, maybe Medea was just saying a brief and proper farewell.

In actuality, she was once more engaged in saving the young hero's posterior. This time there was no traffic in magic embrocations. Medea merely gave Jason a tip in basic psychology. Jason, who it was quite clear by now lacked the heroic wherewithal to make the grade on his own, at least had the sense to recognize good advice. Employing the simple device suggested by Medea, he brought the harvest in on deadline with a minimum of personal effort. He simply threw a stone at one of the men. The man, in turn, thought his neighbor had done it. And in short order all the seed men had turned on one another with their swords until not one was left standing.

Aeetes had no choice but to make as though he'd give the Fleece to Jason, but he still had no intention of doing so. He now committed the tactical error of divulging this fact to his daughter. And Medea, still entranced by the Goddess of Love, confided in turn in Jason. Furthermore, she offered to lead him under cover of darkness to the temple grove where the Fleece was displayed, nailed to a tree and guarded by a dragon. And so at midnight they crept into the sacred precinct of Ares, god of war. Jason, ever the hothead, whipped out his sword, but Medea wisely restrained his impetuosity.

Ares (AIR-eez)

Instead, she used a sleeping potion to subvert the monster's vigilance. Together they made off with the Fleece and escaped to the Argo. Setting sail at once, they eluded pursuit. Thus Jason succeeded in his heroic challenge. And once returned to Greece, he abandoned Medea for another princess. For though Jason had sworn to love and honor Medea for the service she had done him, he proved as fickle in this regard as he'd been unfit for single-handed questing.

Theseus

The Test

It was by lifting a boulder that Theseus, grandson of the king of Troezen, first proved himself a hero. Theseus was sixteen at the time. He had been raised by his grandfather and his mother, Princess Aethra. One day the princess called Theseus to her side. It was time, she said, that he learned of his father, who was the ruler of a mighty kingdom. This was news to Theseus, who had been under the impression that his father was one of the gods. "Before I divulge his identity," said the princess, "you must meet the challenge your father has set you." Years ago, the king had hefted a mighty stone. Underneath he had placed something for his son to find — if he could lift the weight. Aethra guided Theseus to a forest clearing, in the midst of which was a boulder.

Theseus (THEES-yoos or THEE-see-us), Troezen (TREE-zun), Aethra (EE-thra)

The Test (continued)

Theseus proceeded to lift the stone easily, or so the myth is often told. But Theseus would have had trouble with a task involving brute strength. This may be deduced from the tradition that he invented "scientific" wrestling, the discipline by which even a lightweight can beat a stronger adversary by fancy footwork, trick holds and using the opponent's momentum to advantage. Theseus would have had little cause to invent such tactics if he'd been capable of beating his adversaries by sheer physical strength. So when it came to lifting boulders, he was at a disadvantage. Resourcefulness, another heroic trait, must have come to his aid. He would have looked about for some means to multiply his physical strength, perhaps by the principle of leverage.

The Road to Adventure

Beneath the stone Theseus found certain tokens left by his father — a pair of sandals and a sword by which he could prove his identity. His father's name, Aethra now revealed, was King Aegeus of Athens. Prompted by a sense of heroic destiny, Theseus set out forthwith to meet this parent he had never known.

Aegeus (EE-joos)

The Road to Adventure (continued)

He determined to journey to Athens by land, although his mother argued for the safer route by sea. And in fact the landward route proved to be infested by an unusual number of villains, thugs and thieves. Theseus quickly adopted the credo of doing unto these bad guys what they were in the habit of doing to others.

Periphetes

Setting out from Troezen, his birthplace, the first community of any size through which Theseus passed was Epidaurus. Here he was waylaid by the ruffian Periphetes. Periphetes was nicknamed "Club-Man," after his weapon of choice, a stout length of wood wrapped in bronze to magnify its impact upon the skulls of his victims. Theseus merely snatched this implement from Periphetes and did him in with it. Some say that this incident was manufactured to account for depictions of Theseus carrying a club like his cousin Heracles, one of a number of instances on Theseus's part of heroic imitation.

Epidaurus (ep-ih-DAW-rus), Periphetes (per-ih-FEE-teez)

Sinis

The next malefactor who received a dose of his own medicine was a fellow named Sinis, who used to ask passers-by to help him bend two pine trees to the ground. Why the wayfarers should have wanted to help in this activity is not disclosed. Presumably Sinis was persuasive. Once he had bent the trees, he tied his helper's wrists — one to each tree. Then he took a break. When the strain became too much, the victim had to let go, which caused the trees to snap upright and scatter portions of anatomy in all directions. Theseus turned the tables on Sinis by tying his wrists to a couple of bent pines, then letting nature and fatigue take their course.

Sinis (SIN-is)

Sciron

Then, not far from Athens, Theseus encountered Sciron. This famous brigand operated along the tall cliffs which to this day are named after him. He had a special tub in which he made each passing stranger wash his feet. While they were engaged in this sanitary activity, Sciron kicked them over a cliff into the ocean below, where they were devoured by a man-eating turtle. Theseus turned the tables on Sciron, just as he had turned them on Pine-Bender.

Sciron (SKY-ron)

Procrustes

The most interesting of Theseus's challenges came in the form of an evildoer called Procrustes, whose name means "he who stretches." This Procrustes kept a house by the side of the road where he offered hospitality to passing strangers. They were invited in for a pleasant meal and a night's rest in his very special bed. If the guest asked what was so special about it, Procrustes replied, "Why, it has the amazing property that its length exactly matches whomsoever lies upon it." What Procrustes didn't volunteer was the method by which this "one-size-fits-all" was achieved, namely as soon as the guest lay down Procrustes went to work upon him, stretching him on the rack if he was too short for the bed and chopping off his legs if he was too long. Theseus lived up to his do-unto-others credo, fatally adjusting Procrustes to fit his own bed.

Procrustes (proh-KRUS-teez)

Arrival in Athens

When at last Theseus arrived in Athens to meet his father King Aegeus for the first time, the encounter was far from heartwarming. Theseus did not reveal his identity at first but was hailed as a hero by the Athenians, for he had rid the highway of its terrors.

Banquet

In honor of his exploits, he was invited to the palace for a banquet. Serving as hostess was his father's new wife, Medea. This was the same Medea who had helped Jason harvest a crop of armed warriors and steal the Golden Fleece out from under the nose of the dragon that guarded it. Jason had eventually abandoned Medea, and she had grown understandably bitter. Now she sized up Theseus and decided that he was a threat to her own son's prospects of ruling Athens after King Aegeus.

Medea (mee-DEE-uh)

Banquet (continued)

Years before, it was Medea's magic that had ensured the birth of Theseus to Princess Aethra of Troezen. Now Medea played on the king's insecurity. Surely the stranger at the banquet was too popular with the people. He might well seize the throne for himself. The king was persuaded to serve Theseus poisoned wine. And the hero, unawares, would have drunk it had he not paused first to carve his dinner. Or perhaps, more dramatically, Theseus drew his sword not to mince his boar's meat but to reveal his identity. In any case, Aegeus recognized the pattern on the sword's hilt. This was his own weapon, which he had left under a rock for his son to discover. Aegeus dashed the poisoned cup to the ground. Medea stormed out and made her escape in a chariot pulled by dragons.

Tribute for The Minotaur

Theseus was now the recognized heir to the kingdom of Athens. Thus he was on hand when King Minos of Crete arrived to collect his periodic tribute of young men and maidens to be sacrificed to the Minotaur. A monster, half-man, half-bull, the Minotaur lived in the center of a maze called the Labyrinth. The beast had been born to Minos's wife Pasiphae as a punishment from the gods.

Minos (MYE-nos), Crete (kreet), Minotaur (MIN-uh-tawr), Labyrinth (LAB-ih-rinth), Pasiphae (pa-SIF-ay-ee)

Tribute for The Minotaur (continued)

Some say that Theseus expressed his solidarity with his fellow citizens of Athens by volunteering to be one of the victims. Others maintain that Minos noticed the handsome young prince and chose him to be sacrificed. In any case, Theseus became one of the fated fourteen who embarked on the ship to Crete.

A Test

The sea upon which they sailed was the domain of Poseidon, who together with his brothers Zeus and Hades were the three most powerful gods of the Greek pantheon. They divided up creation, Zeus taking the sky, Hades the underworld and Poseidon the sea. But there were other deities of the watery depths, notably the "Old Man of the Sea," with his fifty daughters known as the Nereids. When Theseus was en route to Crete, he encountered one of these divinities. King Minos had made rude advances to one of the Athenian maidens and Theseus sprang to her defense, claiming this was his duty as a son of Poseidon. (Theseus, of course, was also the son of King Aegeus, but a true hero required an immortal father, so Theseus had both.) Minos suggested that if Theseus's divine parentage were anything but a figment of his imagination, the gods of the sea would sponsor him. So Minos threw his signet ring overboard and challenged Theseus to dive in and find it.

Zeus (zyoos or zoos), Hades (HAY-deez), Nereids (NEE-ree-ids)

A Test (continued)

Not only did the hero retrieve the ring from the underwater palace into which it had fallen, but he was given a jewelled crown by one of the Nereids. Not long after he arrived in Crete Theseus encountered another sponsor in the form of Princess Ariadne, daughter of King Minos. She fell in love with him at first sight. It was Ariadne who gave Theseus a clew which she had obtained from the master craftsman Daedalus. In some versions of the myth it was an ordinary clew, which is to say a simple ball of thread. It was to prove invaluable in the quest to survive the terrors of the Labyrinth.

Ariadne (ar-ee-AD-nee)

The Labyrinth

The Labyrinth was a maze so cleverly and intricately contrived by its builder Daedalus that once thrown inside, a victim could never find the way out again. Sooner or later, he or she would round a corner and come face to face with the all-devouring Minotaur. This was the fate which awaited Theseus. It is clear from the myth that the Labyrinth was a maze from which none could escape because it was so diabolically meandering. Hence the Minotaur was not just its monster but its prisoner.

The Minotaur

When Theseus first entered the maze he tied off one end of the ball of thread which Ariadne had given him, and he played out the thread as he advanced deeper and deeper into the labyrinthine passages. Many artists have depicted Theseus killing the Minotaur with his sword or club, but it is hard to see how he could have concealed such bulky weapons in his clothing. More probable are the versions of the tale which have him coming upon the Minotaur as it slept and then, in properly heroic fashion, beating it to death with his bare fists. Or maybe he broke off one of the creature's horns and stabbed him to death with it. Then he followed the thread back to the entrance. Otherwise he would have died of starvation before making his escape.

Escape from Crete

Theseus now eloped with Ariadne, pausing only long enough to put holes in the bottom of her father's ships so that he could not pursue. But Theseus soon abandoned the princess, either because he was bewitched by a god or because he had fallen in love with her sister Phaedra. Some say that he left Ariadne on the island of Naxos, but others maintain that such was his haste that he left her on the small island of Dia, within sight of the harbor from which they had sailed. The deserted and pining Ariadne has been a favorite theme of artists down through the ages. She was eventually rescued by the god Dionysus, who made her his wife.

Phaedra (FEE-druh), Naxos (NAK-sos), Dia (DYE-uh), Dionysus (dye-oh-NYE-sus)

Return to Athens

As the ship bearing Theseus and his liberated fellow Athenians approached the promontory on which King Aegeus watched daily for his return, Theseus forgot the signal which he had prearranged with his father. The vessel's sails were to be black only if the expedition concluded as on all previous occasions, with the death of the hostages. In the exultation of triumph, or in anguish over the loss of Ariadne, Theseus neglected to hoist a sail of a different hue, and King Aegeus threw himself from the heights in despair. Theseus was now both king and bona fide hero, but this did not put an end to his adventuring. On one occasion he visited the Amazons, mythological warrior women who lived on the shores of the Black Sea.

Aegeus (EE-joos)

The Amazons

The Amazons were renowned horseback riders and especially skilled with the bow. They lived apart from men and only met with them on occasion to produce children for their tribe. Some say that Theseus had encountered the Amazons before, on another post-Minotaur adventure in the company of Heracles. Now Theseus visited the Amazons on his own. Their leader, fearless and hospitable, came aboard his ship with a gift. Theseus immediately put to sea and kidnapped her. Unfortunately, the dubious nature of this achievement was matched if not exceeded in another of the hero's quests.

Heracles (HER-a-kleez)

Peirithous

It was the custom in early Greek historical times for the younger sons of noble houses to embark, in the fine sailing months of autumn, upon the honorable occupation of piracy. When Theseus received word that one such pirate and his crew were making off with the royal Athenian herds at Marathon, he raced to the seaside plain. He grabbed the miscreant by the scruff and spun him around to give him what for. But the moment king and pirate laid eyes upon one another, their enmity was forgotten. "You've caught me fair and square," said Peirithous, for this was the pirate's name, and he was of a royal house. "Name your punishment and it shall be done," said he, "for I like the looks of you." The admiration being mutual, Theseus named as penance an oath of perpetual friendship, and the two clasped hands upon it.

Peirithous (pye-RITH-oh-us)

Helen

And so, in the fullness of time, when Theseus decided to carry off young Helen of Sparta, Peirithous agreed to lend a hand. This was the same Helen whose face would "launch a thousand ships" when, as Helen of Troy, the lover and captive of the Trojan Paris, she caused the allies of her husband to wage the Trojan War to bring her home. At the time of Theseus's contemplated abduction, however, she was a mere lass of thirteen. And Theseus, having succeeded in spiriting her off with Peirithous's assistance, left her with his mother for safekeeping while he went about his business and she grew of marriageable age. But before this had come to pass she was rescued by her brothers, the hero twins, Castor and Pollux, whose conjoined starry constellation still brightens the night sky between fellow heroes Orion and Perseus.

Castor (CAS-ter), Pollux (POL-uks),
Orion (oh-RYE-un), Perseus (PURS-yoos or PUR-see-us)

Persephone

One day not long after this escapade, Peirithous drew Theseus aside and spoke to him earnestly. "Remember when I agreed to help you with Helen?" he inquired, "and you pledged to help me in turn in any little outing of a similar nature?" Theseus nodded and muttered yes. "Good," responded Peirithous. "Spoken like a true pal. Well, I've picked my little exploit. I've decided to make off with Persephone, wife of Hades, King of the Dead." Theseus was speechless at the very idea of this sacrilege, but a pledge is a pledge. And so the two set off for the Underworld via one of the convenient caverns leading thereto. And at length they fetched up before the throne of Hades. Lacking any false modesty, Peirithous boldly stated his business, adding that he was sure the god would concede that Persephone would be happier with himself.

Persephone (pur-SEF-uh-nee)

Hades

Hades feigned consent. "Very well," he said. "If you love her that much and you're sure the feeling's mutual, you may have Persephone. But first, join me in a cordial. Please, take a seat." He gestured at a bench nearby, and the two heroes, little thinking it was bewitched, seated themselves upon it. And here they stuck like glue. Meanwhile, Hades loosed a flock of torments upon them in the form of serpents and Furies and the fangs of the hellhound Cerberus.

Cerberus (SUR-buh-rus)

Hades (continued)

And here the two heroes would be stuck today, were it not that Heracles happened to be passing by on one of his Labors. Seeing his cousin Theseus's plight he freed him with one heroic yank, leaving only a small portion of his hindparts adhering to the bench. But Heracles couldn't or wouldn't free Peirithous. And so Theseus's pal pays for eternity the price of his heroic audacity.

Hero of Athens

Some writers in Classical times considered Theseus to have been a historical, rather than a mythological figure. It was even claimed that the episode in the Underworld actually took place in a real-world kingdom. Its ruler, named Pluto (another name for Hades), had a daughter named Persephone and a vicious hound named Cerberus. When the heroes tried to carry off Persephone, her father locked up Theseus and set the dog on Peirithous. Historical or not, Theseus was the national hero of Athens. He was said to have united all the feuding warlords of the Athenian countryside into a federation. He was renowned for his sense of justice and his defence of the oppressed. Escaped slaves taking refuge at his altar in historical times could not be taken back into bondage.

Bellerophon

Exiled

Bellerophon was a citizen of Corinth who was exiled owing to a murder which he had committed. In those days it was possible to be purified of the guilt of such a crime, and Bellerophon was in due course absolved by King Proetus of neighboring Tiryns. It so happened that the king's wife made a pass at the young hero, and when he repulsed her advances she told her husband that it was Bellerophon who made a pass at her.

Bellerophon (buh-LAIR-uh-fon), Corinth (CORE-inth), Proetus (proh-EE-tus), Tiryns (TIR-inz)

The Letter

King Proetus cloaked his indignation, not wishing to violate the sacred obligations of hospitality by doing harm to his guest. But he contrived his revenge by asking Bellerophon to deliver a letter on his behalf to King Iobates of Lycia, his father-in-law. This is somewhat surprising in that writing hadn't been invented yet, except perhaps a rudimentary form used for inventory-keeping. No wonder Bellerophon couldn't make out the meaning of the message he was to deliver. Either that or the letter was sealed — although for that matter "letters" hadn't been invented yet either.

Iobates (eye-OB-uh-teez), Lycia (LISH-ee-a)

The Favor

What the message said was: "Dear Iobates, please do me a favor and kill the person who hands you this." To do so proved impossible, however, as Iobates was bound by the same strictures of hospitality as King Proetus. So instead he feasted Bellerophon for a goodly number of days and nights, until at length he announced that he had a favor to ask of him. Assuming that this had something to do with a return letter to Proetus, Bellerophon may well have been giving thought to establishing the first postal service, when Iobates surprised him with the unexpected nature of his request. Would Bellerophon be so kind as to rid the kingdom of the Chimaera?

Iobates (eye-OB-uh-teez), Proetus (proh-EE-tus),
Chimaera (kye-MEE-ruh)

The Challenge

Not wishing to sugarcoat the challenge, the king went on to describe the Chimaera as a fire-breathing monster directly related to Heracles' nemesis the many-headed Hydra, and Cerberus, watchdog of Hades. The Chimaera had a lion's front, a goat's middle and a snake's tail (or, in some alternative versions of the myth, the heads of these three beasts with some mixture of body parts). In any case, it was truly ferocious.

Hydra (HYE-druh), Cerberus (SUR-buh-rus),
Hades (HAY-deez)

The Campaign

Iobates was hoping to make good on his son-in-law's request to do away with Bellerophon, and he had hit upon the Chimaera as the ideal agent in expediting his young guest's demise. And while one might think that he would have made little of the Chimaera's dangers in order to instill a false sense of security, Iobates had sized up Bellerophon and deduced that he was a sucker for a challenge — the bigger the better. And in fact Bellerophon was pleased at the opportunity to elevate himself from mere postal-delivery person to authentic hero. He immediately began to plan his campaign of attack.

The Strategy

Word was that the Chimaera was virtually impregnable to any ground assault. Others had waded in on foot with spear or sword — to their eternal regret. There was even a rumor of a mounted warrior who had come up short in the encounter, his horse having been blasted out from under him by the Chimaera's fiery breath. With a keen sense of logistics, Bellerophon narrowed down his viable options to an attack either by air or sea. The latter course being out by virtue of the inland nature of the Chimaera's lair, he settled on the aerial option and immediately set out to procure himself a winged steed.

Pegasus

When Bellerophon was still a boy growing up in Corinth, he had yearned to ride the magic horse Pegasus, immortal offspring of the god Poseidon and the Gorgon Medusa. Pegasus was born when the hero Perseus cut off Medusa's head. Like everyone else, Bellerophon had been unable to so much as approach Pegasus. So he sought the advice of the seer Polyeidus.

Pegasus (PEG-uh-sus), Poseidon (puh-SYE-dun), Gorgon (GOR-gun), Medusa (meh-DOO-suh), Polyeidus (pol-ee-AYE-dus)

Athena

Polyeidus suggested that Bellerophon spend the night in the temple of Athena. In a dream, the goddess came to him and gave him a golden bridle. And in the morning Bellerophon found Pegasus drinking at the spring of Peirene and slipped the bridle over his head, rendering him tame and rideable. Thus once more, in manhood, Bellerophon sought out the Corinthian watering hole and his trusty mount, and as he did so he gave thought to the essential issue of armament.

Athena (a-THEE-nuh), Peirene (pye-REE-nee)

Armament

Clearly not just any sword or spear would do in fighting the Chimaera. For starters, a lance would be indispensable   the sort of spear best suited to fighting on horseback. And even a proper lance was no guarantee of victory over so substantial a foe.

The Solution

Again the gods came to Bellerophon's aid, suggesting that a lump of lead affixed to the end of the spear would have a decidedly deadly effect. Firstly, when thrust into the monster's maw, it would cause the Chimaera to gag. And secondly, when melted by the beast's fiery breath, it would trickle down into its innards and cause a fatal case of heartburn.

Victory

So Bellerophon trekked all the way from Lycia to Corinth, located the fountain of Peirene and found Pegasus sipping therefrom. Mounting up, the hero made a much speedier trip back to Lycia, swooped down on the Chimaera's lair and rammed home the secret weapon. And with a great, gasping groan of rage, the Chimaera gave up the ghost.

More Triumphs

Iobates was still determined to do in his guest, so he now sent him to fight a fearsome neighboring tribe. When the hero won the fray with the help of Pegasus, Iobates forthwith dispatched him to fight the Amazons. And when these women warriors proved no match for the divinely aided Bellerophon, Iobates desperately laid a trap, sending his best soldiers to ambush the hero on his way home. They failed of course, so Iobates finally gave in to the inevitable, giving Bellerophon half his kingdom and his daughter's hand in marriage.

Iobates (eye-OB-uh-teez)

Aftermath

There's a story that Bellerophon got his revenge on the wife of King Proetus by taking her for a ride on Pegasus and pushing her off. Be that as it may, the flying horse figured in the hero's own undoing. In later years, Bellerophon was so vain about what he had accomplished that he sought to join the Immortals in their heavenly abode. He was flying up to Mount Olympus when Zeus, angered at his presumption, sent a gadfly to sting Pegasus. The horse threw Bellerophon and he fell to the earth from a great height. For the rest of his days he roamed the land, lame and alone, for no mortal dared befriend him.

Proetus (proh-EE-tus), Zeus (zyoos or zoos)

Perseus

The Oracle

King Acrisius of Argos was warned by an oracle that he would be killed in time by a son born to his daughter Danae. So he promptly locked Danae up in a tower. But the god Zeus got in, disguised as a shower of gold, with the result that Perseus was born. So Acrisius straightaway stuck daughter and infant into a chest and pushed it out to sea. Perhaps he expected it to sink like a stone, but instead it floated quite nicely, fetching up on an island. Here a fisherman named Dictys came upon the unusual bit of flotsam and adopted a protective attitude toward its contents.

Acrisius (a-KRIS-ee-us), Argos (AR-gaws), Danae (DAN-ay-ee), Zeus (zyoos or zoos), Perseus (PURS-yoos or PUR-see-us), Dictys (DIK-tis)

Trouble

Thus Perseus had the advantage of a pure and simple role model as he grew to young manhood. Then one day Dictys's brother, who happened to be king in those parts, took a fancy to Danae and pressed his attentions upon her. "You leave my mother alone," insisted Perseus, clenching a not-insubstantial fist. And the king, Polydectes by name, had no choice but to desist. Or, rather, he grew subtle in the means of achieving his desires.

Polydectes (pol-i-DEK-teez)

The Bride Price

"Okay, okay, don't get yourself into an uproar," he said to Perseus, though not perhaps in those exact words. He put it out that, instead, he planned to seek the hand of another maiden. "And I expect every one of my loyal subjects to contribute a gift to the bride price," he said, looking meaningfully at Perseus. "What have you to offer?" When Perseus did not answer right away, Polydectes went on: "A team of horses? A chariot of intricate devising? Or a coffer of gems perhaps?"

The Boast

Perseus fidgeted uncomfortably. "If it meant you'd leave my mother alone, I'd gladly give you anything I owned — which unfortunately isn't much. Horses, chariot, gems, you name it — if I had 'em, they'd be yours. I'd go out and run the marathon if they were holding the Olympics this year. I'd scour the seas for treasure, I'd quest to the ends of the earth. Why, I'd even bring back the head of Medusa herself if I had it in my power."

Medusa (meh-DOO-suh)

The Challenge

Pausing to catch his breath, Perseus was shocked to hear the silence snapped by a single "Done!"

"Come again?" he queried.

"You said you'd bring me the head of Medusa," Polydectes replied. "I presume you refer to the monstrous Gorgon with snakes for hair and hideous tusks for teeth, the creature so horrible that her very gaze can turn the mightiest hero to stone. Well, I say fine — go do it."

And so it was that Perseus set out one bright October morn in quest of the snake-infested, lolling-tongued, boar's-tusked noggin of a Gorgon whose very glance had the power to turn the person glanced upon to stone.

Gorgon (GOR-gun)

The Gorgon

Clearly, then, Perseus had his work cut out for him. Fortunately he had an ally in Athena, whose divine aid he now sought. The goddess of crafts and war had her own reasons for wishing to see the Gorgon vanquished, so she was eager to advise Perseus. Why, exactly, Athena had it in for Medusa is not entirely clear. The likeliest explanation is that the Gorgon, while still a beautiful young maiden, had profaned one of Athena's temples. For this sacrilege Athena turned her into a monster, but apparently this wasn't punishment enough. Now Athena wanted Medusa's head to decorate her own shield, to magnify its power by the Gorgon's terrible gaze. Athena told Perseus where he could find the special equipment needed for his task.

Athena (a-THEE-nuh)

Directions

"Seek ye the nymphs who guard the helmet of invisibility," she counseled the young hero. And where, Perseus inquired, might he find these nymphs? "Ask the Gray Sisters, the Graeae, born hags with but a single eye in common. They know — if they'll tell you." And where were the Graeae? "Ask him who holds the heavens on his back — Atlas, renegade Titan, who pays eternally the price of defying Zeus almighty." Okay, okay, and where's this Atlas? "Why, that's simple enough — at the very western edge of the world."

Graeae (GREE-ee), Atlas (AT-las), Titan (TYE-tun)

The Gray Sisters

Before sending him off on this tangled path, Athena lent Perseus her mirrored shield and suggested how he make use of it. And while her directions were somewhat deficient as to particulars, Perseus did indeed track down Atlas, who grudgingly gestured in the direction of a nearby cave where, sure enough, he found the Graeae. Perseus had heard the version of the myth whereby these Sisters, though gray-haired from infancy and sadly lacking in the eyeball department, were as lovely as young swans. But he was disappointed to find himself taking part in the version that had them as ugly as ogres.

The Trick

Nor was their disposition any cause for delight. Sure, they knew where the nymphs did dwell, but that was, in a manner of speaking, theirs to know and his to find out. With cranky cackles and venomous vim, they told him just what he could do with his quest. But the hero had a trick or two up his sleeve, and by seizing the single eyeball that they took turns using, he made them tell him what he wanted to know about the location of the water nymphs.

Gear

At length Perseus found the nymphs in Hades, bathing in the river Styx, and got the gear. This consisted of the helmet of invisibility, winged sandals, and a special pouch for carrying Medusa's head once he'd chopped it off. Medusa would retain the power of her gaze even in death, and it was vital to hide the head unless occasion called for whipping it out and using it on some enemy. The god Hermes also helped out at this point, providing Perseus with a special cutting implement, a sword or sickle of adamant. Some add that it was Hermes, not the nymphs, who provided the winged sandals.

Hades (HAY-deez), Styx (stiks), Hermes (HER-meez)

Considerations

Thus Perseus was equipped — one might even say overequipped — for his task. A quick escape would be essential after slaying Medusa, since she had two equally monstrous sisters who would be sure to avenge her murder, and they had wings of gold or brass which would bear them in swift pursuit of the killer. So at least the winged sandals were a good idea. But if this supernatural appliance guaranteed the swiftest of escapes, why bother with a helmet of invisibility, which made it just about impossible for the Gorgons to find you even if you didn't deign to hurry away? Because it makes for a better myth, that's why.

The Gaze

And so Perseus sought out Medusa's lair, surrounded as it was by the petrified remains of previous visitors, and he found the Gorgon sleeping; Yes, even though he had the good old magic arsenal, Perseus was not so foolhardy as to wake Medusa. And even though her gaze could hardly be expected to turn anyone to stone while her eyes were closed, he used the mirrored shield provided by Athena to avoid looking at Medusa directly. (This suggests that you could be turned to stone just by gazing at Medusa, though most versions of the myth have it that it was the power of her gaze that counted.)

Decapitation

Entering, then, somewhat unglamorously into the fray — if "fray" is the right word to describe a battle against a sleeping opponent — Perseus whacked Medusa's head off. At just that instant, the winged horse Pegasus, offspring of Medusa and the god Poseidon, was born from the bleeding neck. Then Perseus donned his special getaway gear and departed victoriously before Medusa's sisters could take their revenge. Though these sisters were immortal, Medusa clearly was not. She died when her head was severed, which required the special cutting implement given to Perseus by Hermes.

Pegasus (PEG-uh-sus), Poseidon (puh-SYE-dun)

Airborn

Even in death Medusa's gaze could turn things to stone, so Perseus quickly stored his trophy in the special sack provided by the water nymphs. And taking wing once more on his flying sandals, he began his return trip. He got as far as Ethiopia when, from his aerial perspective, he spied an arresting sight. Chained to a seaside rock was a beautiful maiden.

Andromeda

Perseus forthwith descended to inquire more closely into this strange situation. The maiden turned out to be the daughter of King Cepheus, whose wife had claimed to be more beautiful than the daughters of the ancient god known as the Old Man of the Sea. For this impertinence, the gods sent a sea monster to ravage the kingdom. An oracle foretold that the king's only hope was to sacrifice his daughter to the beast. Perseus offered to rescue the princess, whose name was Andromeda, in return for her hand in marriage. The king gave his consent just in time, for the sea monster now hove into sight and bore down upon Andromeda's perilous perch.

Cepheus (SEE-fyoos), Andromeda (an-DRAH-muh-duh)

The Sea Battle

Perseus took to the air on his winged sandals. When the beast darted at the hero's shadow on the water, Perseus plunged down and grappled with it, then buried his sword in its shoulder. Repeatedly he stabbed at the scaly flank and tail until the creature spouted seawater mixed with blood. Perseus feared that he could no longer remain aloft on his spume-soaked sandals, so he descended to a rock where he continued to stab at the sea-monster until it finally succumbed. Cepheus and his queen welcomed their savior, and Andromeda, unshackled, was led off to her wedding feast by the weary but satisfied hero.

The Banquet

That night at the banquet Perseus regaled one and all with tales of his prowess, until suddenly there was a commotion at the door. It turned out to be Andromeda's uncle Phineus who, as King Cepheus had omitted to mention, had been promised her hand in marriage. Phineus had brought along a number of allies who supported his prior claim to the princess. Challanges and taunts were exchanged, and then the banquet erupted in bloody warfare. Eventually Perseus was so worn out with hacking and hewing that he resorted to his secret weapon.

Phineus (FYE-nyoos)

The Stoning

"All who are my friends, turn aside your eyes!" he commanded, as he drew Medusa's head from his sack. Amazingly, not one of the enemies was smart enough to heed this tipoff, and at least one ally was dense enough to fail to look askance. Perseus proceeded to turn each and every one of Phineus's cohorts to stone. Phineus himself begged for mercy, claiming that he had acted out of love for Andromeda rather than enmity for the hero. Perseus callously rejected this supplication, stating that his soon-to-be wife would benefit from having a lasting memorial of her former fiancee. Phineus was accordingly frozen forever in a cringing attitude.

Taken for Granite

Meanwhile, back home, King Polydectes had gone back to pestering Danae just as soon as Perseus was out of sight. Returning at last to his mother's rescue, the hero marched boldly into Polydectes' court. There, in cushioned splendor, sat the king surrounded by his sycophants. "Well," he sneered, "what have you brought me?" Perseus produced the bag. "The Gorgon's head, as promised," he replied. "Would you like to see it?" Polydectes made the mistake of saying yes.

Epilogue

The ensuing years of prosperity and contentment for Perseus and Andromeda were somewhat marred by what happened next. Leaving the kindly fisherman Dictys on the throne of the island kingdom, Perseus returned to his native city of Argos. His grandfather heard he was coming and, ever mindful of the oracle's prophesy, left town. Perseus innocently followed. Invited to partake in an athletic contest, he thrilled the crowd with his skill at the discus.

Finale

Unfortunately the wind blew his shot astray and his grandfather, who had joined the audience, was struck in the head (or foot) and died. Eventually Athena immortalized Perseus by placing him in the sky as a constellation, together with Andromeda, her parents and the sea monster.

Odysseus

Background

In the tenth year of the Trojan War, the Greeks tricked the enemy into bringing a colossal wooden horse within the walls of Troy. The Trojans had no idea that Greek soldiers were hidden inside, under the command of the hero Odysseus. That night they emerged and opened the city gates to the Greek army. Troy was destroyed. Now it was time for Odysseus and the other Greeks to return to their kingdoms across the sea. Here begins the tale of the Odyssey, as sung by the blind minstrel Homer.

Odysseus (oh-DIS-yoos)

Book One

"Oh Goddess of Inspiration, help me sing of wily Odysseus, that master of schemes!" So Homer begins his epic, though the hero himself is still offstage. We are treated to a glimpse of life among the supreme gods on Mount Olympus. Urged on by Athena, the goddess of war, they decide that Odysseus has been marooned too long on the island of the nymph Calypso.

Athena (a-THEE-nuh), Calypso (kuh-LIP-soh)

Book Two

Meanwhile, the mansion of Odysseus is infested with suitors for the hand of his wife Penelope. Everyone assumes Odysseus is dead. His son Telemachus calls an assembly to ask for help, and Zeus sends an omen of the suitors' doom. Two eagles swoop down, tearing throats and necks with their talons. Afterwards Telemachus sets sail for the mainland to seek news of his father.

Penelope (puh-NEL-uh-pee), Telemachus (tuh-LEM-uh-kus), Zeus (zyoos or zoos)

Book Three

Telemachus consults King Nestor, who led a contingent in the Trojan War when he was in his nineties. Nestor tells what he knows of the Greeks' return from Troy: "It started out badly because of Athena's anger. Half the army, your father included, stayed behind at Troy to try to appease her. The rest of us made it home safely — all except Menelaus, who was blown off course to Egypt, where he remained for seven years. Seek advice from Menelaus. I'll lend you a chariot to travel to his kingdom."

Nestor (NES-tor), Menelaus (meh-neh-LAY-us)

Book Four

Menelaus tells what he learned of Odysseus while stranded in Egypt after the war. He was advised by a goddess to disguise himself and three members of his crew in seal pelts and then pounce on the Old Man of the Sea. If they could hold him down while he transformed himself into various animals and shapes, he would send them on their homeward way and give news of their companions. Menelaus did as instructed and was informed that Odysseus was presently being held against his will by the nymph Calypso.

Book Five

Zeus, the King of the Gods, sends his messenger Hermes skimming over the waves on magic sandals to Calypso's island. Though the goddess isn't happy about it, she agrees to let Odysseus go. But the raft on which he sets sail is destroyed by his enemy, the god Poseidon, who lashes the sea into a storm with his trident. Odysseus barely escapes with his life and washes ashore days later, half-drowned. He staggers into an olive thicket and falls asleep.

Hermes (HER-meez), Poseidon (puh-SYE-dun)

Book Six

Odysseus awakens to the sound of maidens laughing. Princess Nausicaa of the Phaeacians has come down to the riverside to wash her wedding dress. Now she and her handmaids are frolicking after the chore. Odysseus approaches as a suppliant, and Nausicaa is kind enough to instruct him how to get the king's help in returning to his home. Odysseus follows her into town.

Nausicaa (naw-SIH-kay-uh), Phaeacians (fee-AY-shunz)

Book Seven

Odysseus stops on the palace threshhold, utterly dazzled. The very walls are covered in shining bronze and trimmed with lapis lazuli. The blacksmith god Hephaestus has even provided two brazen hounds to guard the entrance. Odysseus goes right up to the queen and puts his case to her as a suppliant. The king knows better than to refuse hospitality to a decent petitioner. He invites Odysseus to the banquet which is in progress and promises him safe passage home after he has been suitably entertained.

Hephaestus (heh-FEES-tus)

Book Eight

The next day is declared a holiday in honor of the guest, whose name the king still does not know. An athletic competition is held, with foot races, wrestling and the discus. Odysseus is invited to join in but begs off, prompting someone to suggest that he lacks the skills. Angered, he takes up a discus and throws it with such violence that everyone drops to the ground. That night at a banquet, as the court bard entertains with songs of the Trojan War, Odysseus is heard sobbing. "Enough!" shouts the king. "Our friend finds this song displeasing. Won't you tell us your name, stranger, and where you hail from?"

Book Nine

"My name is Odysseus of Ithaca, and here is my tale since setting out from Troy. We sacked a city first off, but then reinforcements arrived and we lost many comrades. Next we visited the Lotus Eaters, and three of my crew tasted this strange plant. They lost all desire to return home and had to be carried off by force. On another island we investigated a cave full of goat pens. The herdsman turned out to be as big as a barn, with a single glaring eye in his forehead. This Cyclops promptly ate two of my men for dinner. We were trapped in the cave by a boulder in the doorway that only the Cyclops could budge, so we couldn't kill him while he slept. Instead we sharpened a pole and used it to gouge out his eye. We escaped his groping by clinging to the undersides of his goats."

Ithaca (ITH-uh-kuh), Cyclops (SYE-klops)

Book Ten

"Next we met the Keeper of the Winds, who sent us on our way with a steady breeze. He'd given me a leather bag, which my crew mistook for booty. They opened it and released a hurricane that blew us back to where we'd started. We ended up among the Laestrygonians, giants who bombarded our fleet with boulders and gobbled down our shipmates. The few survivors put in at the island of the enchantress Circe. My men were entertained by her and then, with a wave of her wand, turned into swine. Hermes the god gave me an herb that protected me. Circe told me that to get home I must travel to the land of Death."

Laestrygonians (lee-stri-GOH-nee-uns), Circe (SER-see)
Hermes (HER-meez)

Book Eleven

"At the furthest edge of Ocean's stream is the land to which all journey when they die. Here their spirits endure a fleshless existence. They can't even talk unless re-animated with blood.' Accordingly, I did as Circe instructed, bleeding a sacrificed lamb into a pit. Tiresias, the blind prophet who had accompanied us to Troy, was the soul I had to talk to. So I held all the other shades at bay with my sword until he had drunk from the pit. He gave me warnings about my journey home and told me what I must do to ensure a happy death when my time came. I met the shades of many famous women and heroes, including Achilles, best fighter of the Greeks at Troy.

Tiresias (teye-REE-si-us), Achilles (uh-KIL-eez)

Book Twelve

"At sea once more we had to pass the Sirens, whose sweet singing lures sailors to their doom. I had stopped up the ears of my crew with wax, and I alone listened while lashed to the mast, powerless to steer toward shipwreck. Next came Charybdis, who swallows the sea in a whirlpool, then spits it up again. Avoiding this we skirted the cliff where Scylla exacts her toll. Each of her six slavering maws grabbed a sailor and wolfed him down. Finally we were becalmed on the island of the Sun. My men disregarded all warnings and sacrificed his cattle, so back at sea Zeus sent a thunderbolt that smashed the ship. I alone survived, washing up on the island of Calypso."

Sirens (SEYE-rens), Charybdis (kuh-RIB-dis), Scylla (SIL-uh)

Book Thirteen

When Odysseus has finished his tale, the king orders him sped to Ithaca. The sailors put him down on the beach asleep. Athena casts a protective mist about him that keeps him from recognizing his homeland. Finally the goddess reveals herself and dispells the mist. In joy Odysseus kisses the ground. Athena transforms him into an old man as a disguise. Clad in a filthy tunic, he goes off to find his faithful swineherd, as instructed by the goddess.

Book Fourteen

Eumaeus the swineherd welcomes the bedraggled stranger. He throws his own bedcover over a pile of boughs as a seat for Odysseus, who does not reveal his identity. Observing Zeus's commandment to be kind to guests, Eumaeus slaughters a prime boar and serves it with bread and wine. Odysseus, true to his fame as a smooth-talking schemer, makes up an elaborate story of his origins. That night the hero sleeps by the fire under the swineherd's spare cloak, while Eumaeus himself sleeps outside in the rain with his herd.

Eumaeus (yoo-MEE-us)

Book Fifteen

Athena summons Telemachus home and tells him how to avoid an ambush by the suitors. Meanwhile back on Ithaca, Odysseus listens while the swineherd Eumaeus recounts the story of his life. He was the child of a prosperous mainland king, whose realm was visited by Phoenician traders. His nursemaid, a Phoenician herself, had been carried off by pirates as a girl and sold into slavery. In return for homeward passage with her countrymen, she kidnapped Eumaeus. He was bought by Odysseus' father, whose queen raised him as a member of the family.

Phoenician (fee-NISH-un)

Book Sixteen

Telemachus evades the suitors' ambush. Following Athena's instructions, he proceeds to the farmstead of Eumaeus. There he makes the acquaintance of the tattered guest and sends Eumaeus to his mother to announce his safe return. Athena restores Odysseus' normal appearance, enchancing it so that Telemachus takes him for a god. "No god am I," Odysseus assures him, "but your own father, returned after these twenty years." They fall into each other's arms. Later they plot the suitors' doom. Concerned that the odds are fifty-to-one, Telemachus suggests that they might need reinforcements. "Aren't Zeus and Athena reinforcement enough?" asks Odysseus.

Book Seventeen

Disguised once more as an old beggar, Odysseus journeys to town. On the trail he encounters an insolent goatherd named Melantheus, who curses and tries to kick him. At his castle gate, the hero is recognized by a decrepid dog that he raised as a pup. Having seen his master again, the old hound dies. At Athena's urging Odysseus begs food from the suitors. One man, Antinous, berates him and refuses so much as a crust. He even hurls his footstool at Odysseus, hitting him in the back. This makes even the other suitors nervous, for sometimes the gods masquerade as mortals to test their righteousness.

Melantheus (muh-LAN-thi-us), Antinous (an-TIN-oh-us)

Book Eighteen

Now a real beggar shows up at the palace and warns Odysseus off his turf. This man, Irus, is always running errands for the suitors. Odysseus says that there are pickings enough for the two of them, but Irus threatens fisticuffs and the suitors egg him on. Odysseus rises to the challenge and rolls up his tunic into a boxer's belt. The suitors goggle at the muscles revealed. Not wishing to kill Irus with a single blow, Odysseus breaks his jaw instead. Another suitor, Eurymachus, marks himself for revenge by trying to hit Odysseus with a footstool as Antinoos had done.

Irus (EYE-rus), Eurymachus (yoo-RIM-uh-kus)

Book Nineteen

Odysseus has a long talk with his queen Penelope but does not reveal his identity. Penelope takes kindly to the stranger and orders her maid Eurycleia to bathe his feet and anoint them with oil. Eurycleia, who was Odysseus' nurse when he was a child, notices a scar above the hero's knee. Odysseus had been gored by a wild boar when hunting on Mount Parnassus as a young man. The maid recognizes her master at once, and her hand goes out to his chin. But Odysseus silences her lest she give away his plot prematurely.

Penelope (peh-NEH-loh-pee), Eurycleia (yoo-ri-KLEYE-uh), Parnassus (par-NAS-us)

Book Twenty

The next morning Odysseus asks for a sign, and Zeus sends a clap of thunder out of the clear blue sky. A servant recognizes it as a portent and prays that this day be the last of the suitors' abuse. Odysseus encounters another herdsman. Like the swineherd Eumaeus, this man, who tends the realm's cattle, swears his loyalty to the absent king. A prophet, an exiled murderer whom Telemachus has befriended, shares a vision with the suitors: "I see the walls of this mansion dripping with your blood." The suitors respond with gales of laughter.

Book Twenty-One

Penelope now appears before the suitors in her glittering veil. In her hand is a stout bow left behind by Odysseus when he sailed for Troy. "Whoever strings this bow," she says, "and sends an arrow straight through the sockets of twelve ax heads lined in a row — that man will I marry." The suitors take turns trying to bend the bow to string it, but all of them lack the strength. Odysseus asks if he might try. The suitors refuse, fearing that they'll be shamed if the beggar succeeds. But Telemachus insists and his anger distracts them into laughter. As easily as a bard fitting a new string to his lyre, Odysseus strings the bow and sends an arrow through the ax heads. At a sign from his father, Telemachus arms himself and takes up a station by his side.

Book Twenty-Two

Antinous, ringleader of the suitors, is just lifting a drinking cup when Odysseus puts an arrow through his throat. The goatherd sneaks out and comes back with shields and spears for the suitors, but now Athena appears. She sends the suitors' spearthrusts wide, as Odysseus, Telemachus and the two faithful herdsmen strike with volley after volley of lances. They finish off the work with swords. Those of the housemaids who consorted with the suitors are hung by the neck in the courtyard, while the treacherous goatherd is chopped to bits.

Antinous (an-TIN-oh-us)

Book Twenty-Three

The mansion is purged with fire and brimstone.
Odysseus tells everyone to dress in their finest and dance,
so that passers-by won't suspect what has happened.
Even Odysseus could not hold vengeful kinfolk at bay.
Penelope still won't accept that it's truly her husband
without some secret sign. She tells a servant to make up
his bed in the hall. "Who had the craft to move my bed?"
storms Odysseus. "I carved the bedpost myself from
the living trunk of an olive tree and built the bedroom
around it." Penelope rushes into his arms.

Book Twenty-Four

The next morning Odysseus goes upcountry to the vineyard where his father, old King Laertes, labors like a peasant. Meanwhile, the kin of the suitors have gathered at the assembly ground, where the father of the suitor Antinous fires them up for revenge. Odysseus, his father and Telemachus meet the challenge. Laertes casts a lance through the helmet of Antinous' father, who falls to the ground in a clatter of armor. But the fighting stops right there. Athena tells the contending parties to live together in peace down through the years to come.

Laertes (lay-ER-teez)

Made in the USA
Las Vegas, NV
30 November 2024